MOTOCROSS

Carmel Reilly

Motocross

Text: Carmel Reilly
Publishers: Tania Mazzeo and Eliza Webb
Series consultant: Amanda Sutera
Hands on Heads Consulting
Editor: Kirstie Innes-Will
Project editor: Annabel Smith
Designer: Leigh Ashforth
Project designer: Danielle Maccarone
Permissions researchers: Lumina Datamatics
Production controller: Renee Tome

Acknowledgements
We would like to thank the following for permission to reproduce copyright material:

Front cover: Gerain0812/Shutterstock.com; p. 4: istock.com/vm; p. 5: Parilov/Adobe Stock Photos; p. 6: Heritage Images/Hulton Archive/Getty Images; p. 7: Keystone-France/Gamma-Keystone/Getty Images; p. 8: Classic-Ads/Alamy Stock Photo; p. 9: All Canada Photos/Alamy Stock Photo; p. 10: DPPI Media/Alamy Stock Photo; p. 11: (top left) NurPhoto/Getty Images; (top right) Independent Photo Agency Srl/Alamy Stock Photo; (bottom left) ZUMA Press, Inc./Alamy Stock Photo; (bottom right) UPI/Alamy Stock Photo; pp. 12,13: (top) iStock.com/Grassetto; (bottom) iStock.com/Rawpixel; p. 14: (left) movetheuniverse/Shutterstock.com; (right) imageBROKER.com GmbH & Co. KG/Alamy Stock Photo; p. 15: (top left) FotograFFF/Shutterstock.com; (top middle) iStock.com/avid_creative; (top right) iStock.com/andreonegin; (bottom left) Remus Kotsell/E+/Getty Images; (bottom middle) Radharc Images/Alamy Stock Photo; (bottom right) pbpgalleries/Alamy Stock Photo; p. 16: LightField Studios/Shutterstock.com; p. 17: Parilov/Shutterstock.com; pp. 18, 19: MarVil/Shutterstock.com; p. 20: Georgii/Adobe Stock Photos; p. 21: LuisMPerez/Shutterstock.com; p. 22: (top) Sirbouman/Alamy Stock Photo; (bottom) Gareth Kelley/Alamy Stock Photo; p. 23: (left), (title page) iStock.com/simonkr; (top right) iStock.com/js-k_de; (bottom right) dolah/iStock/Getty Images; p. 24: Volodymyr Melnyk/Alamy Stock Photo; p. 25: (top) iStock.com/StockPhotoAstur; (bottom left) Baptiste Fernandez/Icon Sport/Getty Images; (bottom right) Cal Sport Media/Alamy Stock Photo; p. 26: (left) Frank Bienewald/Alamy Stock Photo; (right) Edu_2ev/Shutterstock.com; p. 27: (top left) iStock.com/vm; (top right) Wirestock, Inc./Alamy Stock Photo; (middle) Kalman/Shutterstock.com; (bottom) PROMA1/Shutterstock.com; p. 28: (top) MediaNews Group/Inland Valley Daily Bulletin via Getty Images/Getty Images; (bottom) Jose Antonio Lopez 1971/Shutterstock.com; p. 29: (top) OlegRi/Shutterstock.com; (bottom) (back cover) iStock.com/ermess; p. 30: Frank Bienewald/Alamy Stock Photo; graphic representations of bikers: Irkhamsterstock/Adobe Stock Photo.

NovaStar

ISBN 978 0 17 033519 5

Cengage Learning Australia
Level 5, 80 Dorcas Street
Southbank VIC 3006 Australia
Phone: 1300 790 853
Email: aust.nelsonprimary@cengage.com

For learning solutions, visit **cengage.com.au**

Printed in China by 1010 Printing International Ltd
1 2 3 4 5 6 7 29 28 27 26 25

Nelson acknowledges the Traditional Owners and Custodians of the lands of all First Nations Peoples. We pay respect to Elders past and present, and extend that respect to all First Nations Peoples today.

CONTENTS

WHAT IS MOTOCROSS?

Motocross is a high-energy motorcycle sport that takes place on dirt tracks and features tight turns, dips and jumps. It is an extreme sport, full of thrills and action. From start to finish, riders compete not just with each other but with the challenging track as well. Motocross often attracts large crowds, too. **Spectators** love watching the race, especially seeing the riders perform their **daredevil** leaps and turns.

Motocross riders often leap high into the air as they navigate the tracks.

Since its beginnings more than a century ago in the United Kingdom (UK), motocross has become popular all over the world. No matter where you live, the basics required for riders are always the same: a motorbike, good protective gear and a decent level of fitness. Attempting to control a motocross bike is challenging, so riders need to be fit and strong!

While most people take part in motocross for fun, some people go on to compete in major competitions, nationally and internationally. Some of these riders become **professionals**, turning a fun pastime into a full-time job.

Many children around the world learn motocross.

MORE THAN A CENTURY OF RACING

Motocross emerged as a sport in the early twentieth century, when motorcycles were becoming an increasingly popular form of transport. Riders set up clubs and participated in races and **time trials**, often travelling to **rural** areas to test out their bikes.

Motorbikes in the 1910s looked more like bicycles with motors than the modern bikes we see today.

These basic bikes were used in the first dirt track events in the UK in the early 1900s. The first official off-road race on a dirt track, or "scramble" as it was known then, took place in the UK in 1924.

After World War II, motocross riding spread across Europe. In 1947, the first international motocross event was held in the Netherlands. In 1952, the first European championships were held in the UK. By the 1960s, the sport was also becoming popular in countries such as the USA, Australia and Aotearoa New Zealand. In 1972, the American Motorcyclists Association began their own American Motocross Championships.

WHAT'S IN A NAME?

The term "motocross" has been used since the 1920s. It is a combination of the French word for motorcycle, "*motocyclette*", and the term "cross-country".

These riders were taking part in an international motocross race in France in 1956.

New-Look Bikes

Before the 1950s, people used similar kinds of motorcycles for on-road and off-road racing. However, as on-road bikes became heavier and more powerful, new kinds of off-road bikes were developed. These bikes were lighter and more **flexible** to suit bumpy **terrain** and the unpredictable nature of dirt tracks.

Japanese bike makers, such as Yamaha, have made most bikes since the 1960s.

MOTOCROSS TODAY

Today, motocross is the most popular motorcycling sport. There are thousands of motocross clubs and private tracks around the world where people can learn and compete.

Motocross sporting associations exist in more than 100 countries around the world, including Australia, Belgium, India, Aotearoa New Zealand, the UK and the USA. The Fédération Internationale de Motocyclisme (FIM, or International Motocross Federation), based in Switzerland, is the sport's international **governing body**. It organises international racing events, promotes safety and encourages the inclusion of women and young people in the sport.

Motocross is popular with both boys and girls.

MOTOCROSS COMPETITIONS

Lots of different kinds of motocross championships are held around the world, drawing large crowds.

World Championships

The largest competitions in the world are the FIM World Championships and the AMA (American Motocross Association) Championships. Both competitions have a men's and a women's category.

A championship tournament takes place over a year. In the USA, the AMA holds 12 races across the country. The FIM has 18 events held in Europe and other parts of the world. In 2024, races were held in Argentina, Indonesia and China. In 2025, Australia was one of the hosting nations. In both competitions, riders are awarded points for each of the races they take part in. The person with the highest points overall at the end of the year is declared the champion.

Championship races are fast-paced and thrilling.

COURTNEY DUNCAN

Women's FIM World Champion

New Zealand rider Courtney Duncan started motocross when she was seven. By the age of 14 she knew she wanted to be a professional. In 2019, at 23, she became the women's world champion. Since then, Courtney has won the title a further three times!

RICKY CARMICHAEL

AMA Motocross Champion

American rider Ricky Carmichael is one of the best motocross riders of all time. He began competing professionally at the age of 16. Between 1997 and 2007, Ricky won 15 championships in the USA.

THE MOTOCROSS BASICS

The two essential elements of motocross are the motorcycles and the tracks they are ridden on.

Motocross Motorcycles

Motocross motorcycles are specifically designed for riding on motocross tracks. Motorcycle **manufacturers** make different sizes and styles of bikes to suit riders of varying ages, sizes and strengths. Many riders also make changes to bikes themselves to make them more comfortable or faster to ride. Bikes can also be modified for people with disabilities.

Compared with road bikes, motocross bikes are lighter and more flexible. They have many features that make them perfect for riding on difficult terrain. Special **forks** and **shock absorbers** allow jolts from the bumpy surface of the tracks to be less intense. They are part of the bike's **suspension system**.

MOTOCROSS MOTORCYCLE

Weight: *40–100+ kg*

Seat: *Narrow and forward sloping, so rider can easily rise and stand*

Tyres: *Narrow with deep **treads** for riding over rough ground*

Brakes: *Less powerful as bikes are lighter and travelling more slowly*

ROAD BIKE

Weight: *100–200+ kg*

Seat: *Wider and padded for long rides. Can also take a passenger.*

Tyres: *Smooth, wide and rounded for paved roads*

Brakes: *More powerful. Strong brakes are needed to stop heavier bikes, which travel faster and in busy traffic.*

Motocross Motorcycles vs Road Bikes

Tracks

Motocross tracks are **circuits**. They range from 1.5 to 5 kilometres in length and have natural surfaces of dirt, sand or clay. Most tracks use the natural form of the existing terrain to create the bends and ups and downs of the course. All tracks are designed to challenge riders and create maximum thrills, and they have many features in common. However, because terrains everywhere are so different, no two motocross tracks will ever be the same.

Each of these tracks poses different challenges to riders.

Common features of a motocross track
TABLETOP
STARTING GATE
WHOOPS
DROP OFF
S CURVE
SINGLE JUMP

STAYING SAFE

Motocross is an extremely active sport. While it is exciting, it can also be risky. Riders need to be as safe as possible to avoid accidents and to lessen any damage when they do have an accident. Riders can look after themselves by having a good level of fitness, learning how to ride well and wearing protective gear.

Fitness

One of the best ways to stay safe on a bike is by keeping fit. Motocross is a very energetic sport and bikes are powerful. A good rider needs to be fit, strong and flexible in order to keep control of their bike. Exercising and playing sports, building up muscles and stretching are a part of a rider's **routine**.

Motocross riders need to stay fit and strong.

Safe Riding

Riders must always be mindful of others while racing, too. For example, when entering a track, riders should always check for other bikes. And, when racing, riders should not move across the track, but stay in the same line, or position on the track, to allow other riders to pass.

Riders should make sure their bikes are always in good condition and well maintained. This helps to reduce breakdowns on the track, which could cause accidents.

Riders need to remain aware of bikes on either side of them to avoid accidents.

Protective Gear

HELMETS

All riders must wear motocross full-face helmets. They protect riders from head and face injuries. They also provide shade from the glare of the sun.

GOGGLES

Goggles are essential to shield riders' eyes from wind, dust and flying objects, such as small stones thrown up by other bikes.

GLOVES

These are made of stretchy but sturdy fabric that allows movement but also stops hands from rubbing on the handlebars and protects against falls.

BOOTS

Motorcross boots help guard feet, ankles, shins and calves. Feet are vulnerable in accidents. Because feet are used to steady riders as they take corners, they need to be well covered.

BODY ARMOUR

Many riders also use extra protective armour such as neck braces, knee braces, chest protectors, and elbow and hand guards.

JERSEY

These tops protect riders from sunburn and scratches. They are lightweight and easy to move in.

PANTS

Motocross pants are made of heavy but flexible material that does not tear easily. They have **reinforced** areas around the hips and knees that also help the rider grip the bike with their legs.

HOW TO RIDE LIKE A PRO

To ride like a professional, riders need to have good riding posture and know how to handle corners and jumps. The best way to achieve this is to get lessons from an experienced teacher, but the tips below will give new riders a few ideas about what they need to do.

Riding Posture

"Posture" means the position in which someone holds their body. Having a good riding posture in motocross is essential. It not only allows a rider to have more control over their bike, but also means fewer accidents and injuries.

Good posture is essential to avoid falling from the bike in the air.

To achieve good posture on a bike, a rider needs to remember:

1. to ride leaning forward with their head in line with the handlebars and their elbows angled upwards. Their back should be straight and their **core** strong.
2. to aim to spend more time standing than sitting. When they are standing, the balls of their feet should be on the **footpegs** and their knees should be bent. This position helps the rider to control their bike and move with it at the same time.

This rider is using good posture to handle the track.

Handling Corners

1. When going round corners, riders should brake and lean forward as they approach the corner, keeping their elbows out and their head up.
2. Riders should stay in the same "lane" they are already in and not cut across the corner in front of other riders.
3. They should lean the bike, but not their body, into the corner. Their core should be strong. The inside leg and foot should be held up and out from the bike.
4. Riders should accelerate slightly as they round the corner.
5. They should accelerate more as they come out of the corner and then put their inside foot back on the footpeg.

Leaning the bike into the corner helps the rider to avoid a fall.

This rider will start to accelerate more as they finish the corner.

Taking Jumps

1. When taking jumps, riders should stand with their knees slightly bent and the inside of the knees gripping the fuel tank.
2. They should hold their elbows out from their body and keep their head up to look at the upcoming jump.
3. Riders should keep the bike on a straight path and their acceleration even as they jump.

Having the correct posture for jumping is essential.

The rider must hold the the bike straight in the air.

4. Riders should keep gripping with their knees as the bike flies through the air.
5. Riders should land on the back wheel and, as the front wheel comes down, accelerate to keep moving forward on the track.

The back wheel always comes down first after a jump.

STARTING OUT

Access to tracks and training is different in different places and countries. For many people, the best way to start out in motocross is to join a club, find a local track or take lessons.

Motocross Clubs

In many countries, motocross clubs are at the heart of the sport. Club membership allows access to at least one track and places to practise, race and meet other riders. Clubs often offer riding lessons and some hire out bikes and safety gear. Children and teens under 18 years of age need to be accompanied by a parent or guardian.

Adults make sure that children learning motocross stay safe and learn the basics before tackling harder skills.

Tracks, Classes and Coaches

In some places, rather than joining a club, people pay to use private tracks. Many track owners also hire out bikes and provide classes or coaching. People with their own bikes can hire private coaches.

Local Races

Local clubs and tracks hold racing events most weekends, with categories for different age groups and bike sizes. As riders gain confidence, many begin to take part in regional competitions, which can then lead to national competitions. The best riders often join large professional motocross teams to compete internationally.

Local clubs are a great way to improve at the sport.

JETT LAWRENCE

Motocross Champ

Australian rider Jett Lawrence started out competing locally, but soon moved into international competitions. At the age of 11, he won the FIM Junior Motocross World Championship title in Europe. In 2018, when he was 15, Jett moved to the USA, where he has since won several titles in the AMA Motocross and Supercross Championships.

LEARNING THE LINGO

Motocross has its own kind of lingo, or language, that people taking part in the sport frequently use. These terms are used to describe features of the sport, such as parts of the track and types of riding. Here are just a few key terms.

HARDPACK

When the track surface becomes hard, and often slippery.

WHIP

Moving the back of the bike sideways while jumping.

BERM

A large banked, or steeply angled, corner on a track.

DRAGON BACK

A ski-jump style jump that looks like a dragon's back.

CARVE

Riding through a corner or berm at high speed, without tyres slipping. Sometimes called "holding the inside line".

ON THE PIPE

When a rider is going very fast.

IN THE WEEDS

When a rider is forced off the track due to their own mistake or by another rider.

PEEWEE

A 50cc motorcycle.

HIT A HOLESHOT

The first person to get to the first corner in a race and be in the early lead.

STACKING

Crashing.

SCRUB A JUMP

Stay low in the air while jumping to make the jump faster.

WASH OUT

When the front tyre slips going around a corner, making the rider fall.

WHOOPS

A series of small hills, to be ridden over as fast as possible.

DOUBLE JUMP

When a rider flies over two jumps at once.

MOTO

An individual race.

MOTOCROSS SPIN-OFFS

Supercross

Supercross is similar to motocross, but instead of using outdoor tracks it is run on specially made dirt tracks inside stadiums. Having less space means the tracks are shorter, narrower and have more twists, turns and steep jumps.

More than 150 riders race at one time in supercross.

Enduro

Enduro racing takes place on long cross-country courses with lots of challenges for the rider. Most enduro races are trials against the clock, where a rider is expected to complete a part of the ride in under a certain time. Races can be very long, sometimes continuing over several days, and may have many stages.

Enduro riders might have to race for 3 to 4 hours at a time.

Supermoto

Supermoto combines three different kinds of tracks: dirt surfaces, jumps and paved roads. Supermoto bikes are similar to motocross bikes, but their suspension is less springy, and they have smaller wheels and smoother tyres to cope with the different conditions.

Supermoto race tracks include paved roads as well as off-track sections.

Freestyle and Big Air

In Freestyle and Big Air, riders perform daredevil tricks in front of a judging panel, who award them points. Riders jump from ramps or between ramps. As they fly through the air, riders will do one or two tricks, such as flipping or turning their bikes or pivoting away from their bikes.

POPULAR TRICKS

A superman – the rider brings their legs up behind them so they are flying horizontal to the bike.

An airplane – the rider lets go of the bars with one hand.

A 360 – the rider and bike do a full spin in the air.

This rider is performing a 360.

MARVELLOUS MOTOCROSS

Motocross is a demanding sport that requires fitness, skill and dedication. It's also a thrilling sport to take part in and to watch.

Although riding motorbikes can be risky, motocross is a sport that emphasises safety and wearing protective gear.

Many riders start riding at a young age and go on to compete in international events all over the world.

It is a sport with a lot of fans who enjoy watching the excitement of motocross races and the thrilling tricks.

Spectators love watching motocross events.

Glossary

circuits (*noun*)	roughly circular routes that start and finish at the same place
core (*noun*)	the centre of the body
daredevil (*adjective*)	daring or dangerous
flexible (*adjective*)	easy to bend without breaking
footpegs (*noun*)	part of a motorbike you push your foot against
forks (*noun*)	the parts of bikes connecting their front wheel to the frame
governing body (*noun*)	a group of people responsible for running something
manufacturers (*noun*)	companies who make something in bulk, usually in factories
professionals (*noun*)	people who are paid to do a sport
reinforced (*adjective*)	made stronger by adding material
routine (*noun*)	a set of actions performed regularly
rural (*adjective*)	to do with the country
shock absorbers (*noun*)	devices that absorb or lessen the impact from jolts
spectators (*noun*)	people who watch what is happening, such as a race or sports competition
suspension system (*noun*)	parts of a vehicle designed to absorb up and down movements
terrain (*noun*)	land or ground
time trials (*noun*)	races in which people try to get the fastest time
treads (*noun*)	the texture (or feel) of tyres

Index